Trucks

HERBERT S. ZIM & JAMES R. SKELLY

ILLUSTRATED BY STAN BIERNACKI

WILLIAM MORROW AND COMPANY

NEW YORK

BY THE SAME AUTHORS
Cargo Ships
Hoists, Cranes, and Derricks
Machine Tools

A Rogewinn Book

Printed in the United States of America.
Library of Congress Catalog Card Number 75–107973

ISBN 0-688-26565-0 (pbk.)

1 2 3 4 5   77 76 75 74

Today trucks are in use everywhere. Even in countries with few cars, trucks are common. They may be seen on the roads of every nation, carrying the products of sea, forest, factory, and farm to market. At the same time trucks take nets to the fisherman, food to the lumberjack, machinery to the factory worker, and chemicals to the farmer. They also wait at the railroad freight station and the shipping terminal to receive the cargoes of train and ship.

3

Modern truck transportation is only as good as the road system. Where cities are connected by high-speed highways, quick and reliable trucking is to be found. Where the roads are poor, truck service is also poor. In the United States and Europe great highway systems have been built, and trucks have become the backbone of land transportation.

Trucks also are carried piggyback on railroad flatcars and on roll-on, roll-off cargo ships. In this way truck lines are extended far beyond the reach of the local highways.

However they travel, trucks have three main parts. First is the chassis (pronounced chassy), the wheeled frame that supports the engine and body. Second is the body,

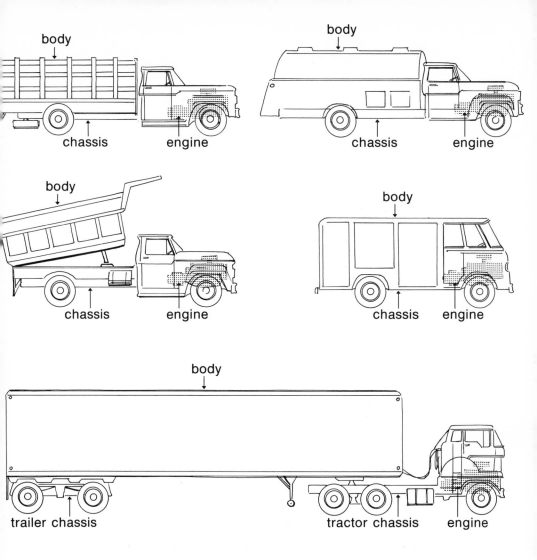

which is attached to the chassis and carries the load. Third is the engine, or power unit, which turns the wheels.

Two long, strong steel beams are the foundation of the chassis. Several cross-pieces tie them together. Below, connected by springs, are the wheels and their axles. Fuel tanks and an air tank, for operating the brakes, are welded to the framework. The chassis must be strong enough to support the engine, cab, body, and the load that the truck will carry. Also it must not sway or twist when the brakes are applied suddenly at highway speeds.

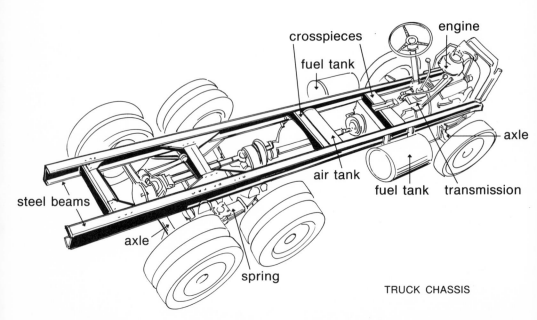

TRUCK CHASSIS

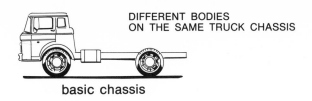

DIFFERENT BODIES
ON THE SAME TRUCK CHASSIS

basic chassis

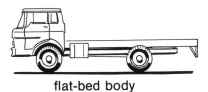

flat-bed body

delivery van body

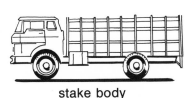

stake body

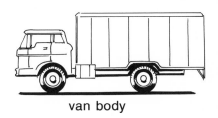

van body

Chassis are built in truck factories, and there are several basic types and sizes. Each may be used with half a dozen or more types of bodies, and each can be powered by several sizes of engines. Extra wheels and axles may be added to the chassis for heavier loads, and a variety of additional equipment for special jobs is available.

7

The two main truck designs are the straight trucks and tractor trailers. Straight trucks have a single chassis on which the wheels, body, cab, and engine are mounted. Tractor trailers have two chassis. One is short and supports the cab, engine, and wheels. This section is called the tractor. The other is much longer and has no engine. It supports the load-carrying section, which is called the trailer. Trailers may be designed for heavy loads like steel bars or

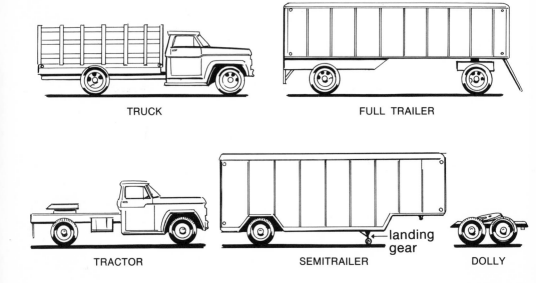

TRUCK FULL TRAILER

TRACTOR SEMITRAILER DOLLY

for light loads like empty cartons. Tractors are built for all-around use. The same one may be used for heavy or for light loads.

Tractors pull full trailers and semitrailers. Full trailers have wheels at the front and back; semitrailers have wheels at the back only. The tractor holds up the front end. When a semitrailer is parked without a tractor, a support called a landing gear is used to hold up the front end.

Truckers call semitrailers "semis." A semi can be converted into a full trailer by putting a "dolly" under the front end. A tractor may pull both a semi and a full trailer. The rig then is called a "double bottom."

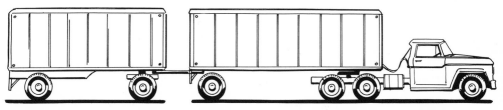

"DOUBLE BOTTOM" TRACTOR TRAILER

A tractor connects quickly and firmly to whatever kind of trailer it is pulling by means of a fifth wheel. This device is a heavy, round, hinged plate behind the tractor cab. When the tractor is backed against the trailer, the steel kingpin in the trailer floor slips into the notch of the fifth wheel and locks into place. The trailer, safely attached, can turn freely behind the tractor.

fifth wheel

kingpin

Truck and trailer bodies are made by companies that specialize in this work. The trucker buys the chassis that is best for the body that will go on the truck. The body must fit the kind of hauling the trucker wants to do.

Bodies are made of plywood, aluminum, steel, or fiber glass, with steel or aluminum framing and supports. The body is bolted firmly to the chassis. There are many body styles to choose from. A body designed for shipping suits or dresses is very different from one that will carry steel bars or haul 5000 gallons of gasoline.

11

PISTON OF GASOLINE AND DIESEL ENGINES TURNS A CRANKSHAFT.

BURNING GASES PUSH FAN BLADES TO TURN A TURBINE SHAFT.

Engines for modern trucks must be powerful, cheap to run, and built to last a long time. Three kinds of truck engines—gasoline, diesel, and gas turbine—are available. All three kinds use the push of burning, expanding gases to turn a shaft. In gasoline and diesel engines, pistons moving up and down in cylinders turn a crankshaft. In turbine engines, a fan spins a rotor shaft. Any of these engines will fit the chassis of a truck or tractor.

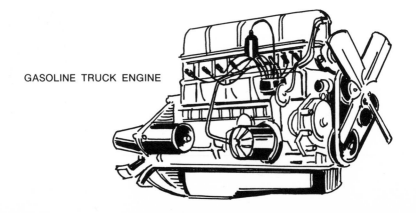

GASOLINE TRUCK ENGINE

In the gasoline engine, gasoline vapor mixed with air goes into the cylinder. The air-gas mixture is compressed by the upstroke of the piston. An electric spark explodes the mixture, driving the piston down and turning the crankshaft. As the piston goes down, another cylinder fires, driving the crankshaft farther around. At the bottom of the piston's downstroke, an exhaust valve opens at the top, and the burned gas goes out through it. When the piston reaches the top again, an intake valve opens. The air-gas mixture is drawn in as the piston goes down. Then the four-stroke cycle starts again.

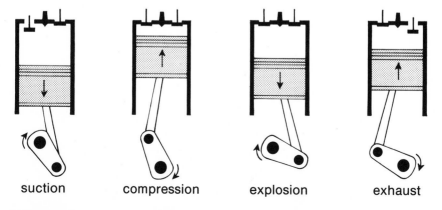

suction   compression   explosion   exhaust

In the diesel engine, air in the cylinder is compressed by the piston. As air is compressed, it gets hot. When the air is hottest, the fuel is sprayed into the cylinder. The diesel fuel explodes, driving the piston down and turning the crankshaft.

Diesel engines work best when they run at steady speeds for a long time, so they are used mostly on heavy-duty, long-distance trucks and tractor trailers. However, a diesel truck costs about a third or a quarter more than a gasoline truck with the same chassis. Besides the higher en-

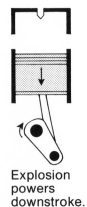  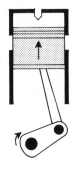 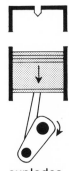

| Explosion powers downstroke. | Air in cylinder is heated by compression. | Fuel injected under pressure | explodes starting next cycle. |

2-STROKE DIESEL ENGINE

gine cost, diesel trucks need heavier gears and shafts because their engines have a more powerful stroke than gas engines. On the other hand, diesel engines last longer and cost less to run and maintain.

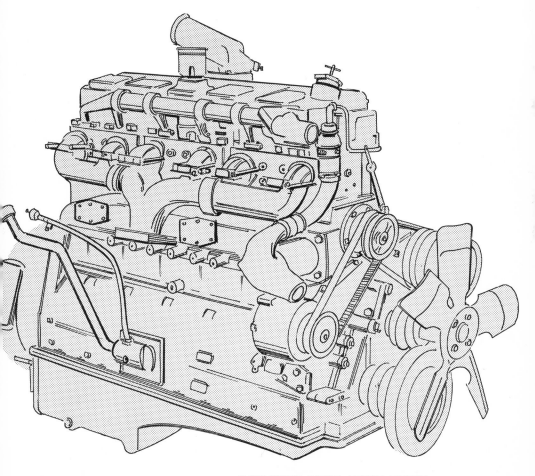

6-CYLINDER DIESEL TRUCK ENGINE

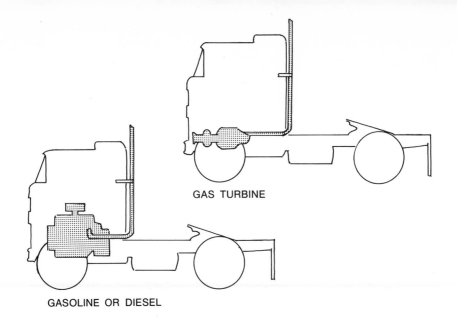

GAS TURBINE

GASOLINE OR DIESEL

The gas turbine is a newer kind of truck engine. Experts say it will replace gasoline and diesel engines. The gas turbine has fewer moving parts and runs more smoothly. It can burn such low-cost fuels as kerosene, liquefied petroleum (LP) gas, or cheap jet fuel, and it causes less air pollution. Two men can lift a gas turbine readily, but at least six men are needed to pick up a heavy-duty diesel.

16

In the gas turbine, burning, expanding gases press against the blades of a rotor, spinning it and its shaft. The whirling shaft turns reduction gears, reducing the speed but increasing the power of the shaft, which goes to the transmission.

These very expensive engines require little service and last much longer than the trucks they power. When the truck body and chassis wear out, the turbine is removed and used in a new truck.

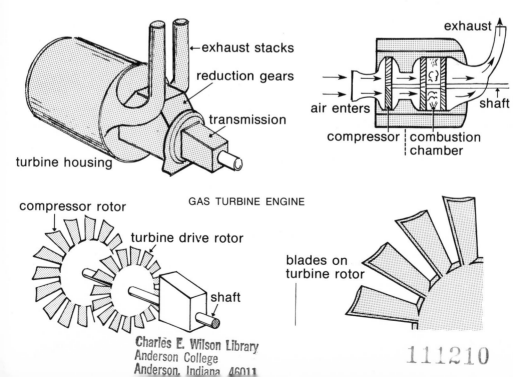

← exhaust stacks

reduction gears

transmission

turbine housing

exhaust

air enters

shaft

compressor | combustion chamber

compressor rotor

GAS TURBINE ENGINE

turbine drive rotor

blades on turbine rotor

shaft

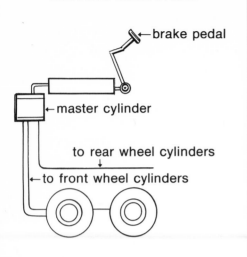

brake pedal

←master cylinder

to rear wheel cylinders

←to front wheel cylinders

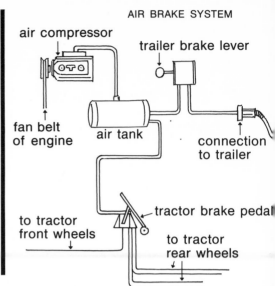

air compressor

trailer brake lever

fan belt of engine

air tank

connection to trailer

to tractor front wheels

tractor brake pedal

to tractor rear wheels

Two kinds of brakes—hydraulic and air —bring trucks to a stop. Hydraulic brakes are used on light trucks. Air brakes, which are more powerful, are used on heavy trucks. On tractor-trailer rigs, the trailer brakes are connected to the tractor by air hoses between the cab and the front of the trailer. The controls for trailer brakes are located on the steering column or the dashboard of the tractor.

18

Learning to use air brakes is not easy. They are so powerful that, if not applied properly, they can lock the wheels, skidding the rig and tearing the tires. If the steering wheel is turned sharply while braking, the trailer may keep going forward faster than the tractor, swinging the rig into a jackknife and out of control. The driver always must brake the trailer first when going forward or downhill and the tractor first when backing or going uphill.

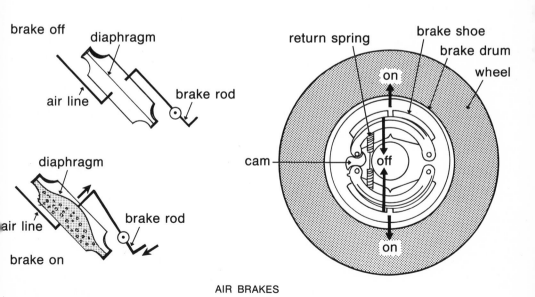

AIR BRAKES

The gearshift lever in the tractor cab controls the gears in the transmission. These gears make the wheels turn at different speeds while the engine runs at a fairly constant rate. To get a heavy load

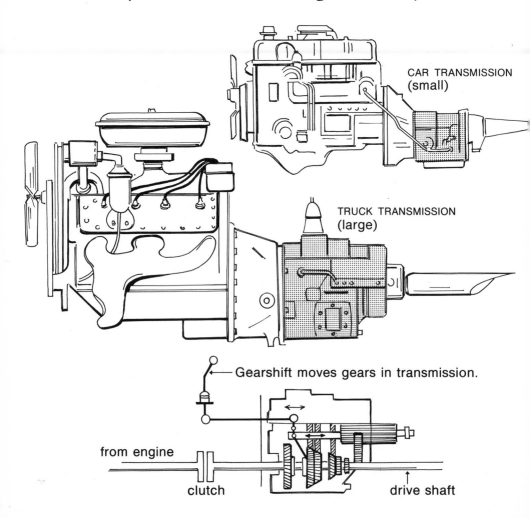

CAR TRANSMISSION (small)

TRUCK TRANSMISSION (large)

Gearshift moves gears in transmission.

from engine

clutch

drive shaft

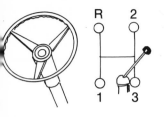

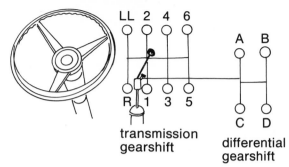

transmission
gearshift

differential
gearshift

moving, or to pull it up a steep hill, low gears are used. On the highway, where the driver wants more speed and needs less power, high gears are used.

Big tractor trailers may have twenty or more forward gears. Such transmissions are very complicated, and shifting them smoothly takes great skill. Nevertheless, almost all truck transmissions are shifted by hand. The driver steps on the clutch and moves the gearshift. If trucks were equipped with automatic transmissions, the engine would burn more fuel.

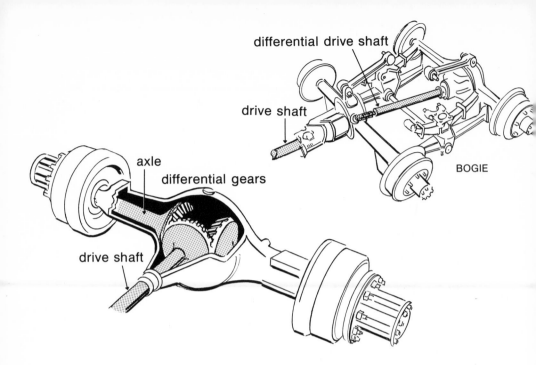

differential drive shaft

drive shaft

axle

differential gears

BOGIE

drive shaft

The differential gears in the axles are turned by the drive shaft. These gears distribute the power evenly from the transmission to the wheels. They are needed, because inside wheels rotate less than outside wheels on a turn. On heavy trucks, a double differential, called a "tandem" or "bogie," is used. A short drive shaft connects the two differentials.

The rear axles on a truck usually have double wheels, and front axles have single wheels. However, some trucks may have as many as 10 wheels, or even more. Trucks can be grouped by the number of wheels (or axles) supporting the load and the number of wheels (or axles) that are supplied with power.

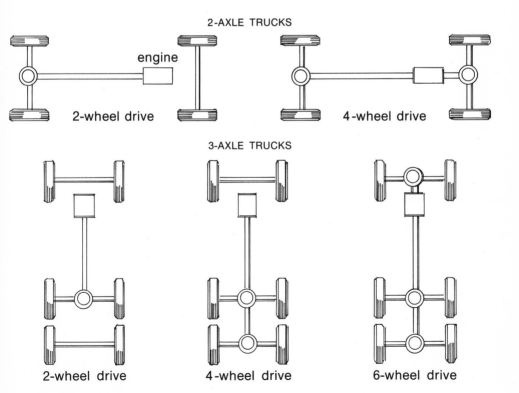

2-AXLE TRUCKS

engine

2-wheel drive

4-wheel drive

3-AXLE TRUCKS

2-wheel drive

4-wheel drive

6-wheel drive

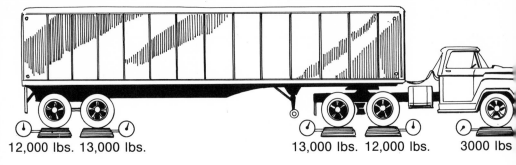

12,000 lbs. 13,000 lbs.   13,000 lbs. 12,000 lbs.   3000 lbs

TOTAL WEIGHT OF TRACTOR, TRAILER, AND LOAD IS 53,000 LBS.
THE LOAD IS SHARED BY ALL THE AXLES OF THE RIG.

Each wheel shares the weight of the truck and the cargo. If some carry more of the load than others, then the tires, brakes, and bearings will wear unevenly. To avoid this problem, a trailer may be equipped with adjustable bogies, which can be moved backward or forward. In this way the weight is distributed equally to all wheels of the rig.

Whether a large truck or small, straight truck or tractor trailer, the driver controls his vehicle from the cab. The cab of a small

24

truck may be as simple as the average car. But the cab of a large diesel tractor looks like the cockpit of a jet plane. It is a maze of levers, pedals, switches, gauges, meters, and indicator lights. The driver needs to learn how to operate them all if he is to drive safely. When he has 30 tons of freight behind him traveling at 70 miles an hour, he must be able to do the right thing without hesitation.

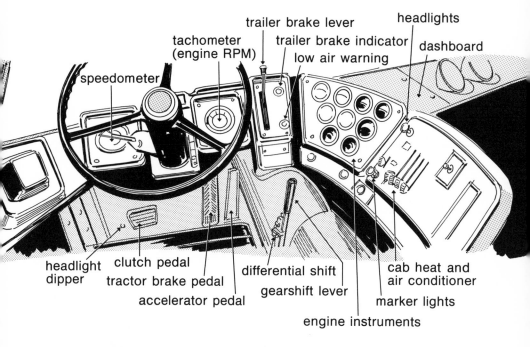

CARAVAN   VAN

Of all the different kinds of trucks, the most common and best known is the box-like van. It is suited for shipping many kinds of freight, and both trucks and tractor trailers may be equipped with van bodies.

The name van comes from the one-horse wagon, called a caravan, that gypsies and circus people once used as a mobile home. Modern vans are made of sheet steel or aluminum. Most are a complete box with roof, floor, and sides. But some have open tops that can be covered with a canvas or plastic tarpaulin.

26

Trailer vans are from 20 to 44 feet long. The larger ones can carry loads that weigh up to 60,000 pounds. Some are made with special types of racks or other fittings. Look inside a big moving van when you have a chance. It is especially fitted to pack furniture tightly and safely for a long haul.

MOVING VANS HAVE SPECIAL FITTINGS
TO SECURE FURNITURE.

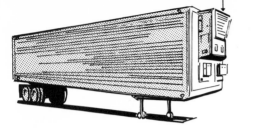 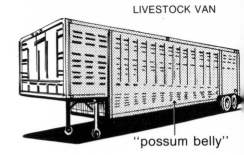

"possum belly"

Refrigerated vans haul chilled or frozen cargoes. The walls are insulated with plastic foam. Look for the refrigeration unit on the front of the van, just behind the cab. These vans haul such perishable cargo as fruit or vegetables from Florida and California to New York and Chicago.

Livestock vans have slots in the sides to let fresh air blow through. Vans for smaller animals like pigs or sheep may have three or more floors, or layers. Those for cattle have only two. Because they often have a low center section, these trucks are called "possum-belly vans."

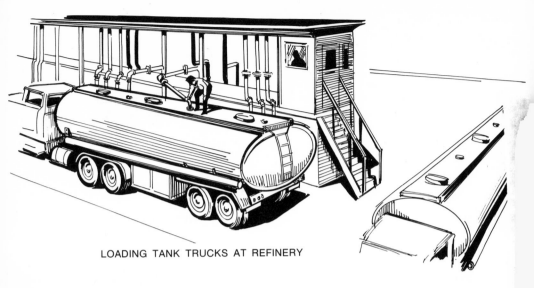

LOADING TANK TRUCKS AT REFINERY

Tank trucks and tank trailers haul liquid cargoes, such as oil, gasoline, kerosene, and other fuels. They come in many shapes and sizes—mainly round or oval.

Some tank trailers are as long as 40 feet, and they can carry as much as 10,000 gallons of liquid. Quick to load and unload, they usually carry cargo one way and return empty for another load.

Dairies use glass-lined tank trucks to

30

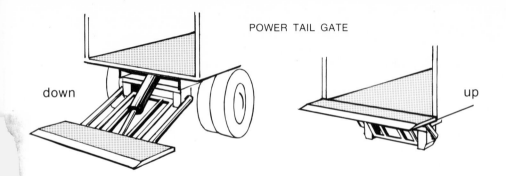

POWER TAIL GATE

down

up

The location of the doors on a van varies according to the cargo it is designed to carry. Some vans load from the back, some from the curb side. Some have locked doors, some just a chain gate. Many vans have a power tail gate. With it, the driver can raise or lower freight from the truck to the street at the touch of a lever.

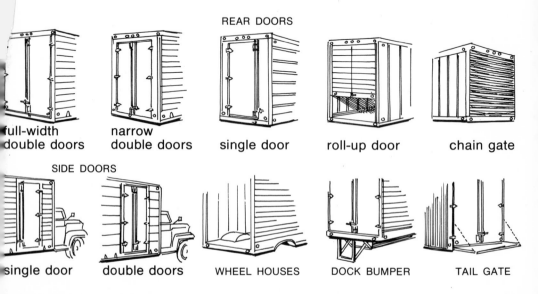

REAR DOORS

full-width double doors

narrow double doors

single door

roll-up door

chain gate

SIDE DOORS

single door

double doors

WHEEL HOUSES

DOCK BUMPER

TAIL GATE

haul milk. Other tank trucks haul liquid fertilizer, insecticides, and weed killers to the farmer. Special tankers deliver solvents, drugs, paints, nail polish, liquid air, ink, and powders from the factories to packaging plants.

Tank trailers usually are made of steel or aluminum. For carrying such edible liquids as salad oil or syrup, they may be lined with plastic or glass. Refrigerated tankers transport milk, orange juice, and drugs. Heated tank trailers are used for

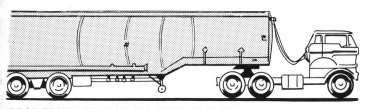

DROP-FRAME CYLINDRICAL TANK TRAILER

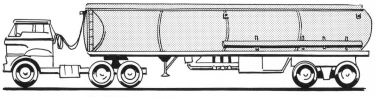

ELLIPTICAL TANK TRAILER

products such as melted chocolate and hot tar. If the tank truck will be hauling acid, lye, or other dangerous liquids, it is built so that it will not break or leak even in a collision or a spill.

High-pressure tank trucks that carry liquid oxygen, rocket fuel, liquid air, or LP gas are painted white to reflect the sun's rays. Otherwise, the solar heat might explode the gas inside. These trucks must be driven with special care, to avoid accidents.

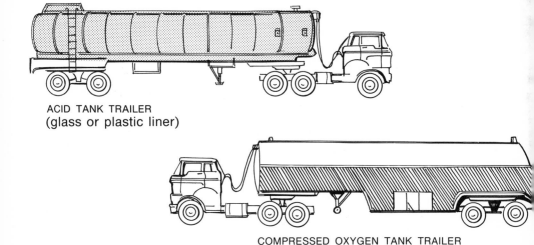

ACID TANK TRAILER
(glass or plastic liner)

COMPRESSED OXYGEN TANK TRAILER

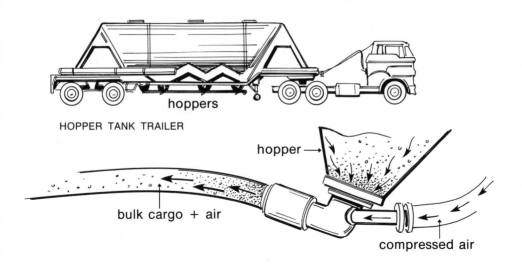

hoppers

HOPPER TANK TRAILER

hopper →

bulk cargo + air

compressed air

A special type of tanker is the hopper trailer. Cement, dry chemicals, salt, wheat, and dry fertilizer are transported in these trucks. Compressed air pushes the fine-grained cargo through large pipes and hoses in a few minutes, to load and unload.

Hopper trailers come in several sizes. They are as long as 35 feet, and the largest can hold as much as 1500 cubic feet of a powdered product, enough to fill an average room right to the ceiling.

block or brick truck   pulpwood truck

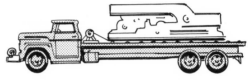

machinery moving truck

Flatbed, or platform, trucks haul large or very heavy objects. They can be loaded from the sides or from above. The bed of these trucks or trailers is made from heavy timbers set over steel beams and cross members. The edges of the bed are protected by steel binding. Platform trucks must stand heavy use. They deliver such cargoes as machinery, steel beams, and bricks. In wet weather, a tarpaulin is wrapped around the load to protect it.

34

The pole trailer is used for carrying long pieces, such as bridge sections, or telephone poles. It has two platforms, connected by an adjustable steel pole.

Rack trailers are used to deliver products like drain tile, cement pipe, or pulpwood. The high, strong end racks keep the cargo from rolling off.

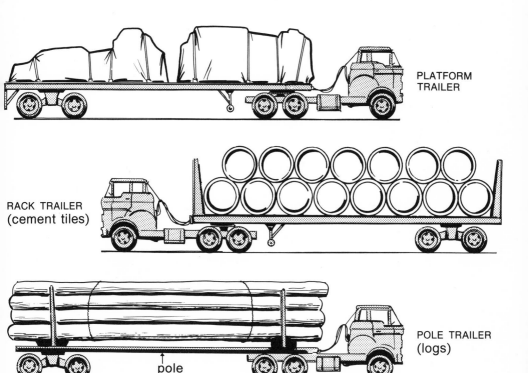

PLATFORM TRAILER

RACK TRAILER
(cement tiles)

POLE TRAILER
(logs)

pole

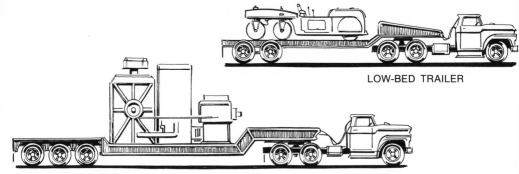

LOW-BED TRAILER

DROP-FRAME LOWBOY TRAILER

The low-bed trailer, called a "lowboy," carries the heaviest loads of all. It has a sturdy frame and up to 22 wheels to support the big loads it hauls. Sometimes the body of a lowboy is only a few inches off the road, so it can handle a taller load. For very heavy loads, a special tractor is used. The tractor may have a winch and steel cables to help load and unload machinery, power transformers, or road rollers, some of the products that these rigs often transport. A large lowboy can carry as much as 120,000 pounds.

In the last few years, the trucking of containers also has become important. Containers, of varied forms, are trucks without wheels. They can be carried on flat trailers, ships, railroad cars, and even on giant new airplanes.

Containers, most of which look like trailer bodies, come in standard sizes that fit together. The most common size is 20 feet long by 8 feet high and 8 feet wide, but there are many variations. These containers can be coupled together to form units 40 feet long, 8 feet high, and 8 feet wide, which can be handled and stored easily.

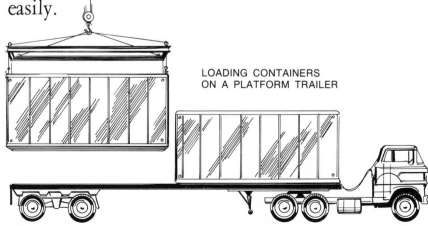

LOADING CONTAINERS
ON A PLATFORM TRAILER

When a TV factory in Japan sends 400 TV sets to a Chicago mail-order house, the boxes are packed into containers. Each container, which holds about 200 TV sets, is put on a platform trailer and hauled to a nearby rail terminal. There it is loaded on a flatcar going to a container terminal at the port. In some cases the trailer may be driven to the port directly.

At the terminal the container is placed in a sorting yard, until it is loaded with many other containers on a container ship bound for Seattle, Washington. Upon

Yokohama

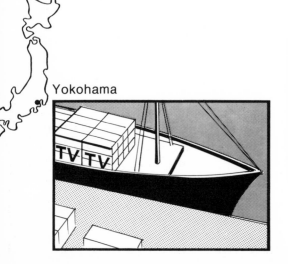

Pacific Ocean

reaching Seattle, the two containers of TV sets are loaded onto platform trailers for the trip to Chicago. Three days later they arrive at the loading dock of the mail-order house. Platform workers unseal the containers and take out the TV sets.

If they had not been shipped in containers, each of the TV sets would have been handled many times by platform workers, stevedores, and longshoremen. Some of the TV sets might have been damaged or lost. By shipping them in containers, however, all arrived in good condition.

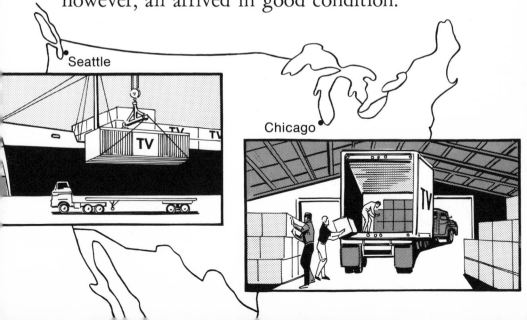

Seattle

Chicago

Containers are available in the same body types as semitrailers. Tank and platform containers have strong end frames so they can be stacked. Insulated containers, designed to transport frozen foods, may have refrigeration units that clip on and keep their contents cold. Hopper containers carry such bulk cargoes as flour and cement.

Standard couplers lock stacked containers together. They can be piled six high at terminals or in the cells of a ship's hold. The capacity of each container is the same as a trailer of equal size.

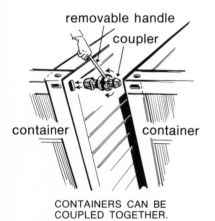

CONTAINERS CAN BE
COUPLED TOGETHER.

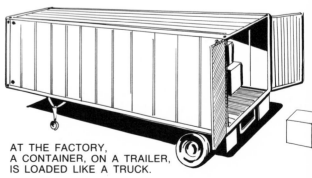

AT THE FACTORY,
A CONTAINER, ON A TRAILER,
IS LOADED LIKE A TRUCK.

Most trucks and tractor trailers used on long-distance hauls are owned by a trucking company. The city terminal is the heart of its operation. A trucking company may have only one terminal or it may have several, but they are all much alike.

Usually a truck terminal has a big parking area for trailers. It often has service areas where tractors and trailers are overhauled, serviced, and repaired. There may be railroad sidings beside the warehouses where freight is stored. Each warehouse has loading docks in front of its wide doors. There the freight is loaded and unloaded. The terminal also has offices for the terminal manager, the dispatcher, and the traffic manager. A high wire fence gives security and protection.

Inside the terminal and its warehouses, freight from incoming trains or trucks is sorted. Pieces going to the same area or the same address are placed together. The traffic department gets the paper work done for each truck or tractor trailer, while it is being loaded. The dispatcher assigns a driver, chooses a vehicle, and decides what time it will leave. The big job is to see that all freight goes to the right place, gets there safely, and arrives promptly.

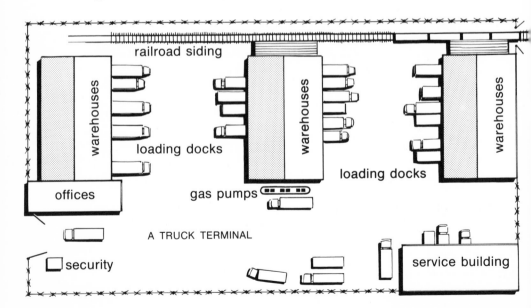

DISPATCHER'S OFFICE

The dispatcher's office is the nerve center of the terminal, for the dispatcher keeps track of each driver and each truck on the road. He knows what is coming in and what is going out—where and when. His office may have many windows so he can see everything that is going on in the yard. Over several busy phones on his desk people report in or ask questions. The dispatcher's job has a lot of pressure.

Platform workers load each truck with care. Heavy pieces are placed on the bottom. The last pieces to be unloaded are put on first. Some loads must be tied down in special ways. By the time the loading is finished, the driver has his orders from the dispatcher. If he is driving a tractor trailer, he brings the tractor down the line to pick up the trailer. As the brakes and lights are hooked up, the driver checks them out.

PLATFORM WORKERS
LOAD THE TRUCKS
AT THE WAREHOUSE.

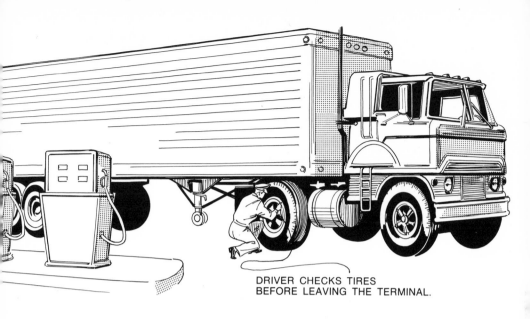

DRIVER CHECKS TIRES
BEFORE LEAVING THE TERMINAL.

By now the driver, his trip ticket in hand, goes over the route carefully. He looks at his papers to be sure he has the right load and destinations. He checks the load, which is then locked and sealed. Now, ready to go, the driver pulls up to the gas pumps. While his tanks are filled he makes one last check of air, oil, tires, brakes, and lights. He climbs in, starts, shifts gears, and moves slowly out to the highway.

45

When the driver gets to the next terminal he tells the maintenance department about anything on his rig that needs attention. The mechanics there fix it if they can. If major repairs are needed, the truck may be sent out to a garage that can do the work. Maintenance departments of large truck lines, however, can do all repair work on the company's trucks. They keep records of lubrication, oil changes, and repairs made on each piece of equipment.

46

If something goes wrong while the truck is out on the road, the driver calls the dispatcher for assistance. Even changing the tires of a big truck is a job requiring two or more men. In any case, the driver seldom works on his rig. Mechanics in truck wreckers, with huge jacks, heavy hoists, and towing equipment, are sent out if the truck has to be jacked up or moved. Another tractor to take the load to its destination may be sent if the tractor is disabled.

CHANGING A TIRE ON A VAN TRAILER

In every large truck terminal, there are thousands of dollars' worth of merchandise, drugs, machinery, electronic equipment, and other valuable goods that are being shipped from one point to another. The trucking company is responsible for these items and must protect them from damage, loss, or theft. With many trucks coming and going at every hour of the day and night, a close check must be kept of everyone and everything that enters or leaves the terminal. The checking is done by the trucking company's security department.

A SECURITY MAN
CHECKS OUT A LOAD OF PIPE.

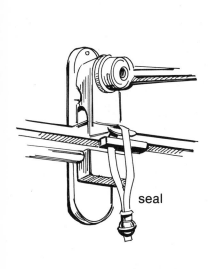

seal

DRIVER AND SECURITY MAN CHECK SEALS
BEFORE TRUCK LEAVES TERMINAL.

Security officers check each incoming and outgoing truck to be sure that it is sealed. To open the doors of the truck, the seal must be broken, so the security officer can tell at a glance if the truck has been tampered with. Security men also patrol the warehouses, loading platforms, and the yard.

49

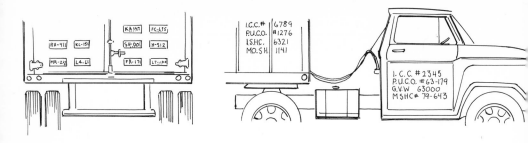

Trucks and tractor trailers often carry several license plates on the back, for they must show the license of each state they drive through. On the side of the cab and on the side and rear of many trailers, there are numbers painted. They indicate that fees have been paid to controlling agencies, such as the Interstate Commerce Commission and the Public Utilities Commissioner's Office.

Truckers pay heavy taxes and fees, sometimes over a thousand dollars a year for a single truck. Since they use and damage the roads more than private drivers, and make a profit from this use, state and Federal governments require them to pay at a higher rate.

Trucks are required to carry marker lights, flares, and other safety equipment. The placement of this equipment is specified by state and Federal regulations. The size and location of rear-view mirrors, windshield wipers, and fire extinguishers are also regulated. If any of them is not in working order, the driver may get a ticket or be pulled off the road until it is repaired.

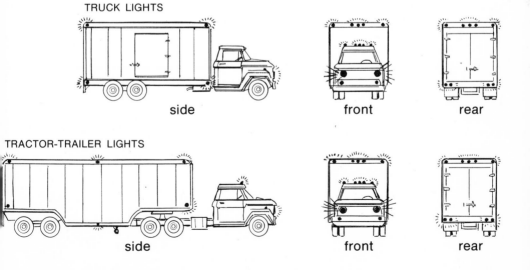

TRUCK LIGHTS

side   front   rear

TRACTOR-TRAILER LIGHTS

side   front   rear

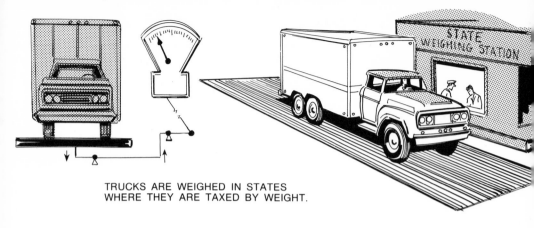

TRUCKS ARE WEIGHED IN STATES
WHERE THEY ARE TAXED BY WEIGHT.

Weight distribution on a truck is important, because if it is uneven the roads may be damaged. Accordingly, each state checks the way the truck is loaded. The states also tax trucks on the load carried on each axle, and most of them limit the overall size of the load.

State weighing stations are located near the borders. Trucks must pull in to be weighed and checked. The driver's papers are inspected to see if taxable freight is entering the state.

To cut costs, truckers would like to put larger trucks on the highways. But lawmakers know that one large truck will be much harder on the roads than two small ones. Safety experts tell us that the larger trucks have greater accident rates than small ones. For these reasons, states limit the size and weight of trucks that use their highways. All states limit trucks to a width of 96 inches, but the length and weight allowed vary from state to state.

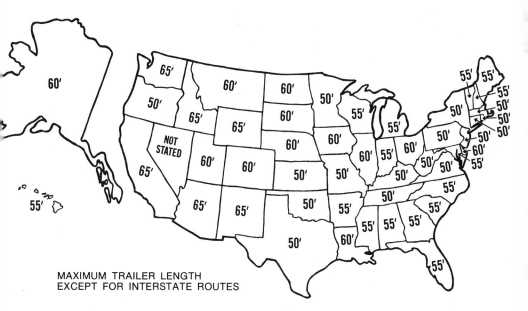

MAXIMUM TRAILER LENGTH
EXCEPT FOR INTERSTATE ROUTES

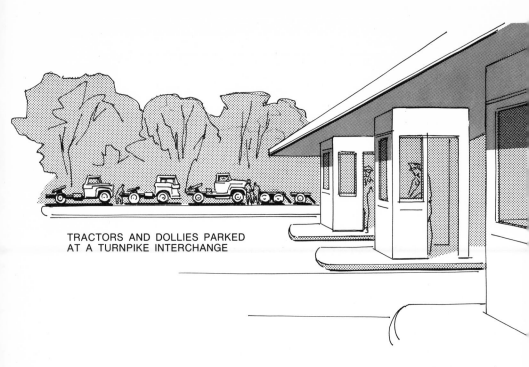

TRACTORS AND DOLLIES PARKED
AT A TURNPIKE INTERCHANGE

Some states allow double-bottom rigs, tractors pulling a semitrailer and a trailer, on interstate routes and turnpikes. When these trucks come off the superhighway, they are met by a tractor that takes the second trailer from there to the terminal. For this purpose, several tractors are kept parked near the exit.

54

When trucks were first built, many years ago, the men who drove them were called teamsters, because they used to drive teams of horses. Many were in the cartage business, delivering shipments from railroads to factories. Some teamsters belonged to a union called the Teamsters Union. Truck drivers, helpers, and warehousemen of today still belong to this union, one of the largest in the United States.

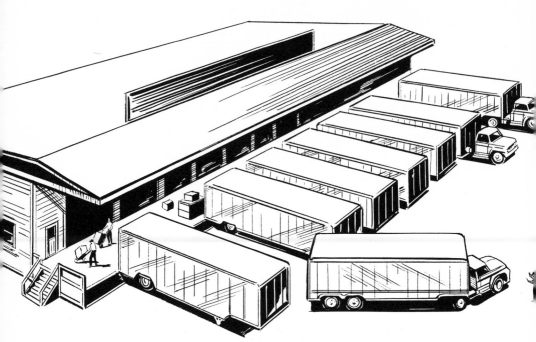

A NEW DRIVER JOCKEYS A TRAILER TO THE DOCK.

Young men who want to be truck drivers often get experience by driving small delivery trucks. They may also start as platform workers in a truck terminal warehouse. There they get a chance to drive trucks around the yard and "jockey" trailers from one dock to another.

When a man has learned to handle big trucks and trailers in the yard, he may be sent out on the road as a driver's helper. In this way he gets practice in highway and city driving and learns the paper work of trucking. When the new driver has passed the test for a chauffeur's license and has enough experience as a helper, he takes a trial run with an expert driver. If he passes this test, he is hired by the company as a driver.

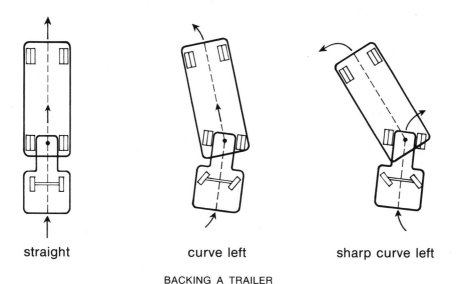

straight   curve left   sharp curve left

BACKING A TRAILER

There are several different sorts of truck drivers. Some are workers who drive trucks as part of some other job. They include repairmen, tradesmen, service men, and firemen.

Another kind of driver takes delivery trucks over short, regular routes. Products such as milk, bread, and mail are distributed in this way. Many of these drivers have other duties besides driving. They sell, collect, or perform services.

Drivers who work for trucking companies operate larger, heavier, and often more complicated trucks. Every day they are responsible for the safe delivery of thousands of dollars' worth of cargo.

The number of hours in one day that a driver may work is specified by the union

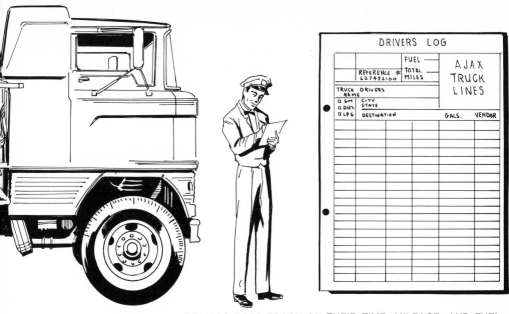

DRIVERS LOG						
		FUEL		A JAX		
	REFERENCE # 627432100	TOTAL MILES		TRUCK		
TRUCK NAME	DRIVERS			LINES		
□ GM	CITY STATE					
□ DIES						
□ LPG	DESTINATION				GALS.	VENDOR

DRIVERS KEEP TRACK OF THEIR TIME, MILEAGE, AND FUEL.

contracts and company policy. Drivers of local trucks work during regular business hours. Road drivers often work odd hours —at night or during times when the traffic on the highways is lightest. These drivers are paid by the hour. They keep track of their time by punching a time clock in the terminals or by keeping a log book with their time in it.

On long trips, two drivers are in the cab. While one drives, the other rests. He can sleep in the bunk built behind the driver's seat, or he can ride in the right-hand seat. There are curtains around the bunk so daylight or headlights will not disturb the sleeper. Drivers split up the work so that each does his share.

ON LONG HAULS, THE DRIVER AND HIS HELPER TAKE TURNS SLEEPING AND DRIVING.

DRIVERS REST AT TRUCK STOPS.

Drivers look forward to the break when they stop for refueling and eating. At special service stations along the major highways, called truck stops, there are gas and diesel pumps, washrooms, and sometimes even showers and beds for the drivers. Each has a restaurant that serves the hearty food drivers like. There the drivers meet and talk about road conditions ahead. The dispatcher even may have a message waiting for one of them.

A ROCKET SECTION IS HAULED ON A LOW-BED TRAILER.

Driving is hard work, but the routine changes from day to day. On a long trip the driver and his helper have to plan their schedule. Road repairs may slow them down; detours may send them over longer routes. Often they are asked to go to new and distant places, with new things to see.

Sometimes a top driver gets an unusual job, like hauling a large machine, a scientific instrument, or a rocket part. On such a trip he may need to know every bridge and underpass on the route to be sure an oversize load gets through safely.

Even though they work hard, truck drivers enjoy driving. They like to sit high in their rigs and hear the tires sing. They are proud of their driving skill, and they know that their job is necessary to our modern way of life.

INDEX